Rest Assured

Seven Days to Stillness, Sanity and the Sabbath You Need

D1248875

Kent A. Murawski

DEDICATION

This book is dedicated to my wife, Gina. Thank you for helping me understand the beauty of slowing down.

REST ASSURED: Seven Days to Stillness, Sanity, and the Sabbath You Need

Published by Kent A. Murawski

www.kentmurawski.com

ISBN 978-0-9981386-3-3
eISBN 978-0-9981386-2-6

Cover Design: Jason Clement

Printed in the United States of America

First Edition 2019

CONTENTS

INTRODUCTION

*D*eath *by overwork.* It sounds funny, doesn't it? The thing is, it's actually true! The term "Karoshi" is a Japanese word meaning, "death by overwork." Traced back to the aftermath of World War II, Prime Minister Shigeru Yoshida was determined to make the rebuilding of Japan's economy his number one priority. He did this by strongly encouraging Japanese corporations to offer lifetime job security and asking their employees for loyalty in return. It propelled Japan into the world's third largest economy today, but it came at a cost. Only a decade after this initiative began, workers from Japan began committing suicide and experiencing strokes and heart failure. The cases were known as "occupational sudden death." One such case happened in 2013 when journalist Miwa Sado of news network NHK allegedly logged 159 hours of overtime in one month and died of heart failure not long after.[1]

Maybe you're not working 159 hours of overtime in month, but chances are you are too busy, and it may *literally* be killing you.

True rest is something that we all desperately need but can't seem to find. By rest, I don't necessarily mean sleep or down time, although that is important. The rest I'm referring to is *rest for our souls.* In the words of the early church father, Augustine of Hippo, "You have made us for yourself, O Lord, and our heart is restless until it rests in you."

Because true rest can only be found in a relationship with God.

Since 2014, God has been teaching me about rest. Over the next seven days, I want to share with you some of what I have learned and take a journey together toward finding true rest.

Here is how it began. In 2009 my family moved to Cambridge,

Massachusetts to start Journey Church. After four years of intense building, God began to lead us on a path to do a launch (similar to a grand opening). Requiring both laser-like focus and intense effort, it was very exciting but also extremely time consuming. In addition to loving my wife, parenting three young children, pastoring the people of Journey Church, and holding down a part-time job as an urban youth worker to make ends meet, we were now attempting this major public launch. Of course, we had an awesome team of people helping to pull it off, but there were still responsibilities that could not be delegated. Looking back, I am not sure how we did it. *It was only by the grace of God.*

During that process, rest was something I learned to fight for. Unnecessary things had to be eliminated in order to concentrate on the things that were most important – my spiritual life, my wife and children, the people of the church, the launch, and my job. During that season, I experienced many sleepless nights, times of crippling anxiety, and days when I could not find rest. Yet through it all, though it would have been easy to come apart at the seams, God sustained me and taught me more about rest than I ever thought possible. I'm still on the journey, learning every day, but these precious truths will remain with me for the rest of my life.

If you feel stressed out, anxious, sleep-deprived, overburdened, burnt out, on the edge of a breakdown, or no matter how much you "rest" you get you don't feel refreshed, then this devotional is for you! If on the other hand you have a great rhythm of rest, I believe this will be a great encouragement to you, and you might even learn something new to deepen your rest in God.

How to Use This Devotional

This is meant to be a seven-day journey. If it takes you longer, that's OK, but try not to do it in less than seven days. Each day ends with a section called, "Selah." It's taken from the psalms and is thought to mean, "pause." The Amplified Bible "pause and calmly think about that." Here are some other tips to help you get the most out of it:

- If possible, find a partner and work through it together. There is strength in partnership, and chances are, you know someone who could benefit from it just as much as you.

- Schedule enough time each day to both read through the devotional and take some time to talk to Jesus about what you read.

- Read slowly and deliberately, recognizing that Jesus is with you. Become more aware of His presence through the process.

- Keep a journal. If you purchased a hard-copy, there is a journal in the back where you can write down your insights for each day. This will allow you to look back on the experience and reflect on what you learned.

If you enjoy the devotional and it adds value to your life, why not let someone else know about it? You can: share it on social media; purchase a copy for someone you know, a small group, or your whole church; or send a direct link to your whole email list to purchase the devotional.

Selah

Throughout this devotional, you will notice the words, "Selah" at the end of each day. Though there is a great deal of uncertainty about what the word actually means, some possible interpretations are "To pause, to weigh in the balance, to praise, to lift up. So in these sections, that's exactly what I want you to do.

Stop, reflect, pray, praise, listen, and obey. Let's start with a prayer.

Father, in Jesus' name, I pray that you would help me to experience your love and presence in a fresh new way and learn how to establish a rhythm of rest that will allow me to live the abundant life You promised. Over the next seven days, please radically transform my heart and teach me to find my rest in You. In Jesus' name. Amen.

DAY 1

THE GIFT OF REST

It all started on a Wednesday afternoon in early April 2014. That particular season had been one of the busiest seasons of my life. At that time, Wednesday mornings were usually spent at home with the kids while my wife went grocery shopping, and Wednesday afternoons were dedicated to prayer. As I mentioned in the introduction, I had been in a season fraught with anxiety. There were so many questions that needed answering and I needed answers yesterday! If you asked me today, I couldn't tell you what seemed to be of paramount importance then, but at the time it felt like life or death. My mind was unfocused, I was irritable and angry - quick to fly off the handle, and my nights were spent tossing with my thoughts in endless streams of consciousness. There was too much weight on my shoulders and I felt like I was drowning.

The apostle Peter told us very simply to cast our anxieties upon Him because He cares for us (1 Peter 5:7), but clearly, I didn't understand how to do that.

That afternoon, I headed downstairs to my home office/guest room to worship and pray. Rather than focusing on Jesus and His goodness, my focus was on getting answers from Jesus. I pressed and strained to hear God. Like Jacob, I was not letting go until God blessed me! I was striving, but instead of finding peace, my heart and mind became more anxious. My thoughts began to turn inward: *Maybe I'm outside of the will of God or have unconfessed sin? Am I living outside the borders of grace in some area of my life? Am I doing things Christ hasn't asked me*

to do and I am reaping the consequences? Whatever it is, please show me Lord! As the tension built, something Jesus said flooded my soul:

> Then Jesus said, "Come to me, all of you who are weary and carry heavy burdens, and I will give you rest. Take my yoke upon you. Let me teach you, because I am humble and gentle at heart, and you will find rest for your souls. For my yoke is easy to bear, and the burden I give you is light." (Matthew 11:28-30 NLT)

At that very moment, the singers on the live web stream from the International House of Prayer began singing that exact verse of Scripture!

Rest Is a Gift to Be Received

God's voice suddenly broke through the swirling chaos, and He said something to me that I will never forget, "You don't have to understand everything happening around you in order to receive My rest."

Rest is a gift to be received.

Immediately, I laid down on the bed and simply began to *receive* from Jesus – His life, His love, His peace, His grace, and yes, His rest! My heart was instantly refreshed, burdens were lifted, anxieties ceased, and Jesus filled my soul with what I was longing for...true rest and peace!

True rest comes when we strive less and receive more from God.

I once heard it said, "We live from God not for God." We live *from* God's rest not *for* God's rest. You can have rest without understanding everything that's going on in your life…if you receive it! Put your agenda to the side and seek Him for who He is.

Jesus is rest.

When we seek Him for who He is, with no other agenda, things begin to come clear, but striving for answers often leads to frustration. Although you may not receive the answer you feel you need at the moment (in my experience it doesn't usually happen that way), God gives us what we really need – Himself!

True rest comes when we stop striving and start receiving from God.

I once heard it said, "We don't live for God, we live from God." We live from God's rest not for God's rest. Stop trying to understand everything that's going on in your life and just receive it. Don't just go to God with your agenda; instead seek Him for who He is and receive from Him. When I seek Him for who He is, with no agenda, things seem to come clear, but when I strive for answers it often leads to frustration.

Although God may not give me the answer I think I need at that moment, He gives me what I really need – Himself. And where God is, there is rest and peace.

Selah

As you begin this seven-day journey of rest, take on a new posture – one of receiving. It may seem foreign to you, or selfish, but try it anyway.

Right now, take a few minutes to lay aside your agenda and simply receive from Jesus with a childlike heart. Receive His love, His grace, His strength and anything else you need, just ask Him. Jesus has given us a standing invitation, "Come to Me, all you who are weary and carry heavy burdens, and *I will give you rest.*" Can you hear it?

And remember, you can't earn rest - it is something Jesus wants to give you as a gift!

DAY 2

THE EXCHANGE

Yesterday, we looked at Matthew 11:28 where Jesus invites us to come to Him and exchange our burdens for His rest. Today, we will continue looking at this promise with a slightly different emphasis.

> Then Jesus said, "Come to me, all of you who are weary and carry heavy burdens, and I will give you rest. *Take my yoke upon you*. Let me teach you, because I am humble and gentle at heart, and you will find rest for your souls. For my yoke is easy to bear, and the burden I give you is light." (Matthew 11:28-30 NLT, italics mine)

Today I want to talk to you about exchanging your burdens for His rest.

My Burnout

There is a built-in alarm system inside of me that goes off whenever I step outside the "borders of grace" or simply put, God's will for my life. It dates back to early 2004. I was very involved at my

5

church...too involved you might say. Is it possible to do *too much* for God? Absolutely! Let me explain. On one particular weekend, I was scheduled to attend a college ministry training event but instead, a few hours before I was set to travel, I crumpled into a heap on the floor and cried like a baby for two hours. I was experiencing a minor nervous breakdown. Obviously, the training was now out of the question – I was a mess, but what instigated this mini-breakdown?

I was operating outside the borders of grace.

Psalm 16 says it superbly, "The boundary lines have fallen for me in pleasant places; surely I have a delightful inheritance" (Psalm 16:6, NIV). After doing the will of God, Jesus was full, not empty. He said, "My food is to do the will of him who sent me and to accomplish his work" (John 4:34).

There is grace from heaven when we are doing the will of God. Oswald Chambers said it best,

> "Whenever there is the experience of weariness or degradation, you may be certain you have done one of two things - either you have disregarded a law of nature, or you have deliberately got out of touch with God."[2]

Whatever I was experiencing certainly didn't feel "delightful." Leading up to that episode, I blew right past the warning signs: sleepless nights, waves of anxiety, feeling down and depressed. This wasn't normal for me. In fact, I had never felt that way before. This wasn't a chemical imbalance; it was a result of poor and uninformed choices on my part that led to burnout.

Over the following weeks and months, Jesus began to talk to me about the state of my life. I had taken on responsibilities that He had not asked me to do. I was wearing a yoke, but not His yoke (at least not all of it)! The responsibilities I had taken on were dizzying. I was newly married, working full-time, pioneering a college and career ministry through our church, and my wife and I were leading the church's entire worship ministry to boot! As I began to seek Jesus about what was happening, He was eager to tell me – *not all the things I was doing were His will.* I had taken on things He had not asked me to do. His voice clearly flooded my soul,

"You didn't get into this mess overnight and you are not going to get out of it overnight." Slowly, over the course of several months, as I let go of some things and focused on Jesus and His will for me, I began to feel healthy again.

Whose Yoke Are You Wearing?

In Scripture, a yoke refers to servitude or obligation. That doesn't sound like a good thing, but the word picture here is beautiful, "Take My yoke upon you. Let me teach you, because I am humble and gentle at heart, and you will find rest for your souls" (Matthew 11:29). The yoke is a collar-like frame fitted to go over the neck and the shoulders of two animals. Jesus is our stronger "older brother" who shoulders the majority of the burden for us. As the late Matthew Henry said, it is not a heavy burden but rather "A yoke lined with love."[3] Taking on His yoke doesn't release us from service, it frees us to walk in relationship - releasing us from the weighty burden of sin and self-effort. Simply put, *Jesus invites us to exchange our burdens for His rest.*

What a great deal. We cash in our weariness, burdens, anxieties, sin and shame for His rest and refreshment! When we take on things that are beyond His will for us, we are operating in our own strength. This is one of the surest ways to burnout. The good is the enemy of the best. So why do we take on yokes or obligations outside of His will for us? Here are a few reasons,

> • Feeling like we need to prove ourselves to God or other people

- Pride that leads us to believe we can do it all on our own

- An upbringing where we had to "pull ourselves up by our "bootstraps"

- A lack of understanding about His will and desire for our lives

- A lack of knowledge about ourselves, our gifts, and our strengths and weaknesses

- Neglecting prayer before taking on new responsibilities

Jesus is inviting us to exchange our burdens for His rest.

Selah

If you are feeling burdened, weary or heavy laden, it could be that you are not wearing His yoke but another not of His making! Take some time today to ask Him about any adjustments you need to make. Write down everything you are currently "doing for God." Pray through the list and ask Him, *is there anything I'm doing that you have not asked me to do? Is there anything I need to let go of? Is there anything not on this list that you would like me to do?*

If you do not feel weary and heavy laden, ask Him to refresh you anyway and take time to receive His rest. It's also good time to re-evaluate His will for your life and to ensure you are in the sweet spot of His will so you can be healthy and effective for His kingdom.

DAY 3

STRETCHED THIN

So much of what we do in life and ministry is focused on others that we sometimes lose sight of our own wellbeing. If you are going to be effective at ministering to other people, you have to learn how to care for yourself. This may sound self-focused or self-serving, but I assure you it's not. Jesus would often draw away by Himself to share life with His Father and be empowered by the Spirit. As leadership guru John Maxwell once said, "To lead others, you must first lead yourself."[4]

As I mentioned previously, like many of you, my life had become overly full. During this time I worried...a lot and became very anxious, to the point where it was disrupting my sleep and daily activities. But I always knew that in those times, I needed to go back to the Source because something was wrong. Something was off. *Aren't I supposed to have peace?* I would ask myself. Maybe you can relate to this, but how do we get out of this rat race?

"Thin, stretched, like butter scraped over too much bread."

I'm a firm believer in taking a Sabbath day. In fact, whenever I violate this principle in an ongoing way, "I feel thin, sort of stretched, like butter scraped over too much bread." That is a quote by Bilbo Baggins from *The Lord of the Rings: The Fellowship of the Ring* by J.R.R. Tolkien. Bilbo goes on to say that he is in need of a very long holiday (vacation).

May I suggest we need a weekly "holiday?" Let's find out what the Bible has to say about the Sabbath.

> On the seventh day God had finished his work of creation, so he rested from all his work. (Genesis 2:2 NLT)

When it says He rested, it means God ceased or stopped. Having such a full schedule has caused me to ask the question, *Can I afford not to take a weekly Sabbath rest?* The obvious answer is no! So what does my Sabbath day look like? I enjoy doing things with my wife and kids like taking leisurely walks or going to the park. Sometimes we go on a special outing or have a family day. Other times we just veg out around the house and watch movies in the middle of the day or play games. I don't check my email, do church work or take phone calls unless absolutely necessary. I try to do things I like and enjoy - putter in the garage, get out my tools, fix something or do projects around the house that I don't normally get to do. Although this may seem like work, for me it's life-giving! Occasionally, I go play golf with some friends (but those of you who have children understand that some of your hobbies must be put on the back-burner for a season).

Taking a Sabbath day once a week helps us to enter His rest on a consistent basis and acts as a built-in reminder to rest.

The point is, a Sabbath day should be restful and life-giving. Taking a

Sabbath day once a week helps us to enter His rest on a consistent basis and acts as a built-in reminder to rest. Remember, when we practice God principles we get God results. You will be better off for taking a weekly Sabbath day.

After all, life shouldn't be all work and no play (or the other way around for that matter). Taking a day of rest gives us space to breath and be rejuvenated so we can be effective for God, our families and others.

Selah

If God Himself rested after His labor, shouldn't we? After all, I'm fairly certain His responsibilities greatly outnumber ours. God didn't rest because He was tired. He rested to ensure we would follow His example because He knew we would need it! If you don't have a Sabbath day built into your schedule, why not pick one now? For many, Sunday is a great day for this. Worship and serve at your church and spend the rest of the day with friends and family doing something rejuvenating.

If you are married, sit down with your spouse to talk and pray together to determine which day it will be and what it will generally look like; what things are OK and what things are off limits. If you are single, sit down with God and talk about it. You won't regret it!

DAY 4

SABBATH

Yesterday, I encouraged you to follow God's example by building a Sabbath day into your weekly schedule. But honoring the Sabbath goes beyond just resting or ceasing from our labor. God also set the Sabbath day apart and calls it *blessed and holy*. So the Sabbath goes beyond the practical to the spiritual.

> And God blessed the seventh day and declared it holy, because it was the day when he rested from all his work of creation. (Genesis 2:3 NLT)

When the Bible says God blessed the seventh day, it means He showered down abundance and fullness on it and filled it with strength. There is a blessing in honoring the Sabbath that comes directly from God!

The passage goes on to say He also, "declared it holy" or sanctified it. It means He set it apart and devoted it to sacred purposes. The Sabbath day was created for honor, refreshment and rest in Him!

The Sabbath Is a Command

That's not all. God takes it step further by making it one of the Ten Commandments.

> Remember the Sabbath day, to keep it holy. (Exodus 20:8 ESV)

This is significant. In other words, it's on the same level as the other Ten Commandments, such as: do not lie, do not steal, do not commit adultery, do not murder etc. Before you get mad and stop reading, let me explain. Christians like to sometimes use the excuse that we are "free from the law" because we are "under grace." I'm not debating that, but grace doesn't free us from the moral law, it gives us a new heart and empowers us to fulfill the law. Jesus Himself said He didn't come to abolish the law or the prophets. He came to fulfill it (see Matthew 5:17)! Most of us would agree *there is no higher law than the law of love*. When we operate by the law of love we will fulfill all the moral law (the Ten Commandments). Love would not steal, kill, lie, or break any of the Ten Commandments because love lives for the good of others. The same way you seek to observe the other Ten Commandments (by grace through faith) you seek to observe the Sabbath day! Loving God and keeping His commands shouldn't be burdensome. God desires it to be a joy (see 1 John 5:3).

The Sabbath Is a Gift

Jesus brings the Sabbath back into focus by telling us it was created for man, not man for the Sabbath day (see Mark 2:27). He takes it from law to grace. The Pharisees were using the Sabbath to oppress and put people under nitpicky obligation. They condemned Jesus and His disciples for "doing work" (they were plucking heads of grain because they were hungry) on the Sabbath. But Jesus beats them at their own game by helping them to see this truth:

The Sabbath is meant to be a gift to mankind, not just another crushing obligation.

It's God-honoring to take care of your basic needs, enjoy Him, do good and have fun on the Sabbath. It was created for your benefit!

When Should I Sabbath?

As the New Testament Christian Church, we generally celebrate the Sabbath on the first day of the week rather than the last day of the week. There is some precedent for this in Scripture and with the early church, but either way, it doesn't matter that much for us. What matters is the Sabbath is a day to rest, be refreshed, experience God's blessing and set aside time to honor, worship and enjoy Him. This would include a Sunday celebration service, serving in your church, and doing good on the Sabbath (feeding the poor, praying for healing, etc) as well as taking some time to just relax, be with family and enjoy the blessings God has given you.

For pastors, it's impossible for Sunday to be our Sabbath. Not that Sundays aren't enjoyable and life-giving; they certainly are or should be. It's often the highlight of my week, but it's also hard work and can be exhausting. Currently, we take our Sabbath on Saturday though we've had to adjust it from time to time. Our whole family does it together. Starting Friday at around 3PM when the kids get home from school, we all work hard to get things done so that from Friday at 5PM to Saturday at 5PM we can rest.

Selah

This might sting a bit, but it needs to be said, not taking a Sabbath rest is prideful, arrogant, sinful and can cause long-term damage in your life. When we don't take time to stop, refresh and honor God, it's like saying, *my work is more important than You and what I have to do takes precedence over your command to rest.*

So, I ask you again, *what day have you chosen for your Sabbath? What is on and off limits that day? How will you honor God on that day?* Let's not let this go one day longer. Like God, take a day of rest. You will never regret it!

DAY 5

A LIFESTYLE OF REST

Over these past several days, I've been giving you building blocks to help you establish a *lifestyle of rest*. The goal is not to take you from zero to hero. *My goal is to help you move just one step each day.* Here are the action points from each day. Let's stop and do a self-evaluation. How are you doing so far? Before moving on, take some time to evaluate:

- Day One – Are you receiving His rest?

- Day Two – Have you exchanged your burdens for His rest?

- Day Three – Have you decided on a Sabbath day and what you will and won't do on that day?

- Day Four – How will you honor God on your Sabbath day?

These are all steps, but if you build them into your life, you will begin a lifestyle of rest that will make you a more focused and effective person for God, your family and others. It's this lifestyle of rest I want to talk about today.

The Promised Land

In the Old Testament, the Promised Land (Canaan) was to be a place of rest and refreshment. They were to inherit land, houses they didn't build, wells they didn't dig and vineyards they didn't plant. The Bible says it was a land *flowing with milk and honey*. That sounds pretty restful to me!

But the Promised Land represented something even greater – a rest that was to come. It foreshadowed a day when Jesus Christ would purchase an eternal rest for His people by giving His perfect life for our sin and rising from the dead to triumph over death once and for all. This rest would restore our weary sin-sick souls back to health by giving us peace with our Creator. Why do we need rest? *Because sin wears people out.* There is a quote many of us have heard that describes it perfectly,

> Sin will take you farther than you want to go, keep you longer than you want to stay and cost you more than you want to pay.

The Promised Land was a future reference to the heavenly rest that all those who are in Christ will experience one day, for eternity.

The Promised Land was a future reference to the heavenly rest that all those who are in Christ will experience one day, for eternity. This life is preparing us to live in God's rest for eternity. Let us not miss Christ's rest because of disobedience.

Three Ways We Can Live in God's Rest, Right Now

1. God's rest is only open to them that believe.

That's exactly what Hebrews 4:3 tells us! Belief also implies obedience. As it turns out those who missed God's rest when they were coming out of Egypt came short due to their unbelief. They didn't combine what they heard (I have a place of rest for you) with faith (obedience). Out of twelve men sent to spy out the land, ten gave a bad report and only two (Joshua and Caleb) had faith and obedience, "Let us go up at once and occupy it, for we are well able to overcome it" (Numbers 13:30 ESV). Joshua and Caleb believed the report God had already given them (see Deuteronomy 1:8) and acted on it.

Let me further illustrate. The hotel where we have our Sunday services sometimes throws us perks. Last year, they gave us four box seats to a Red Sox game and a parking pass for the garage next to the stadium (parking in Boston is a nightmare)! When the head of catering emailed me to let me know, I had to "believe and obey." What if I wouldn't have believed her and had never gone to pick up the tickets? We would not have been able to enter the ballpark, stuff ourselves on hotdogs and popcorn, do the wave with 15,000 other people or sit right behind home plate. We would have missed out!

2. Now is the time to enter God's rest.

Today when you hear his voice, don't harden your hearts. (Hebrews 4:7 NLT).

Some things are time sensitive. When you see a sale going on at your favorite store, you know it will only last just a couple of days or a week at most. If you miss the sale, you have to wait for the next one, but whatever it is you hoped to get may not be there the next time around because *some things simply have an expiration date.* God is merciful, yes, but some things are only for a particular season. If we miss the opportunity it could be gone forever. What am I saying? *Don't wait!* God's rest is meant to be experienced now. It's not that there is no more rest to come, it's just that if you miss the rest He has for you now, you can never get it back. *Now is the time to obey God's voice!*

3. Obeying His commands keeps us in His rest.

So let us do our best to enter that rest. But if we disobey God, as the people of Israel did, we will fall (Hebrews 4:11 NLT).

The opposite is also true. If we disobey God, we lose our rest. "If" is a conditional statement. Rest is contingent upon our obedience. If that's the case, why do we disobey God? Here are a few reasons:

- Fear of the unknown

- His commands seem unachievable (that's because we can't pull them off without His power)

- His promises seem too good to be true and our experience doesn't match up, so we just discount them

- A failure to realize His promise is better and more fulfilling than our current reality

- Refusal to take His promises at face value and walk by faith

So how do we live a lifestyle of rest? It's simple (in theory): *We live in God's rest by believing and obeying in God and His commands.* Obedience doesn't determine your belief it verifies it! Obedience comes out belief. It's not the other way around.

Selah

What have you been putting off? What has God asked you to do that you have not followed through on? Disobedience is burdensome. It causes us to constantly worry because we are at odds with God. Furthermore, if disobedience to His word (the Bible calls it sin) doesn't bother you, something is wrong. In that case, the first step for you would be to *believe* the gospel, obey it, and surrender your life to the care of Jesus Christ. Do a fresh reading of the Romans Road: Romans 3:6, 5:8, 6:6 and 10:9-10, and obey by putting your trust in Jesus Christ to save you from your sins and grant you eternal life.

DAY 6

BE THE TYPE OF PERSON
YOU WANT OTHERS TO BE

Yesterday, we determined that in order to live a lifestyle of rest, we must respond to God in faith and obedience. Today, I want to share with you one of the benefits of rest that isn't about you. Here it is,

Live a lifestyle of rest so you can refresh others.

Life Giving People

Some people are just life-giving. They are fun to be around. When you leave them, you feel encouraged, refreshed and empowered. *They are a breath of fresh air.* I want to be that type of person; one who leaves people better than I find them.

I have a few friends like this. When I'm around them, I just feel refreshed. There is no pressure to be someone I'm not, no pretenses and no masks. They are truthful and honest with me, but when we are finished, I feel refreshed. It comes from a genuine heart of love.

There is a guy in the Bible who was like that. You've probably never heard of him but he encouraged one of the greatest apostles in history. His name was Onesiphorus. Listen what Paul said about him,

> May the Lord bless Onesiphorus and all his family because he visited me and encouraged me often. *His visits revived me like a breath of fresh air*, and he was never ashamed of my being in jail. (2 Timothy 1:16 TLB)

There are people all around you that need a breath of fresh air. Christ has filled you with His life now go give it to others! After all, Jesus didn't come for healthy people, He came for the sick, the weary and the downtrodden (see Luke 5:31-32). Jesus came to make the sick healthy so they could do the same for others!

Jesus came to make the sick healthy so they could do the same for others!

Be the Type of Person You Want Others To Be

Do things on purpose, be generous for no reason, love without cause. In doing so you will revive others and be like a breath of fresh air to them.

> The generous will prosper; those who refresh others will themselves be refreshed. (Proverbs 11:25 NLT)

We all need to be an Onesiphorus and we all need to have an Onesiphorus.

Selah

Don't you think it's time you got started refreshing others? Most of us have way more knowledge than obedience. Why not be generous and give it away? *The challenge today is to refresh one person. Go be an Onesiphorus to someone else!* Bring someone coffee at your workplace for no reason.

Give a compliment just because. Buy your coworkers lunch unexpectedly. Get together with a friend *just to encourage them.* Listen and pay attention to those around you when they share their likes or needs and beat them to it. Go ahead, be the person you want others to be!

DAY 7

EMBRACE THE STILLNESS

People hear God in different ways, many times God speaks uniquely to people based on what He knows they will hear and are able to receive. It could happen while reading the Bible, reading a book, watching a movie or talking with another person. But there is one universal way that God speaks to us. Think about it: He spoke to Moses on the back side of a mountain through a burning bush. He spoke to Gideon while he was threshing wheat in a wine press. He spoke to Samuel in the night hours upon his bed. And they all had one thing in common, *they were in the stillness.*

Be still and know that I am God! (Psalm 46:10 NLT)

I know it's that way for me. It seems like when I slow down long enough to take time embrace the stillness, I hear Him. Stillness and rest go hand in hand. If I don't have times of solitude and stillness I am not really resting in God.

There is a well-known story in the Bible about Elijah the prophet. After three and a half years in exile by a brook where he was fed by ravens Elijah re-enters society. He immediately confronts the wicked king Ahab, kills his wicked prophets, ends a three year drought. By doing so he also earns the scorn of Ahab's evil queen, Jezebel. After this flurry of activity, he is terrified that Jezebel is going to kill him, so he flees to Mt. Horeb (Sinai), i.e. the mountain of God. Elijah is burnt out, disillusioned and just flat out depressed.

He needs to hear God's voice. While there, the Lord sends a mighty wind, an earthquake and fire but it does nothing for Elijah. For all the fanfare, He is still stuck in his despair. But God was setting him up.

> And after the fire there was the sound of a gentle whisper. When Elijah heard it, he wrapped his face in his cloak and went out and stood at the entrance of the cave. And a voice said, "What are you doing here, Elijah?" (1 Kings 19:12-14 NLT)

Elijah heard the voice of the Lord as soon as he arrived on the mountain. God asked him the same question upon his arrival but Elijah didn't *hear* it. I mean, *really* hear it. But after the wind, the earthquake and fire came a gentle whisper and Elijah was ready to not only *hear but obey.* Hearing is nothing without obedience. There is a lot we can learn from that story, but one thing is for certain: *we all need a place where we can be still and hear God.*

Find a Place Where You Can Be Still

Mine changes from time to time and according to the season I'm in. Sometimes it's my home office. Other times it's a special spot in Harvard Square set beside a quaint little fountain. Some days it's as simple as taking a walk. Regardless of where, we must find places where we can be still.

Receive Rather Than Strive

If you remember, on day one we talked about receiving God's rest. We learned that so much of having a relationship with Jesus is learning to receive from Him. We meditate on who He is and enjoy His presence.

Some days you may need some love, other days His strength and every day we need His grace and power. *Whatever we need God has it in abundance and is more than willing to give it.*

Selah

Find a place to take some time and be still today. A place where you can hear and receive from Jesus. *Write down what He says to you.*

List your special places where you can be still and hear God. What did He say to you when you got there?

KENT A. MURAWSKI

CONCLUSION

Over the last seven days, I hope your mindset about rest has changed and you've decided to establish a new rhythm in your life. I am confident that as you practice, you will get better and better at living from a place of rest and find yourself healthier and more alive than ever before!

CONTACT KENT

The best place to connect with me is at www.kentmurawski.com. You can also on find me on social media:

- Twitter Twitter.com/kentmurawski

- Facebook Facebook.com/kentmurawski

- Instagram Instagram.com/kentmurawski

- YouTube channel kentmurawski@gmail.com

- LinkedIn Linkedin.com/in/kentmurawski

DAILY JOURNAL
Day 1

KENT A. MURAWSKI

Day 2

Day 3

Day 4

KENT A. MURAWSKI

Day 5

KENT A. MURAWSKI

Day 6

KENT A. MURAWSKI

Day 7

KENT A. MURAWSKI

Additional Notes

KENT A. MURAWSKI

BIBLIOGRAPHIES

[1] Chris Weller, "Japan is facing a 'death by overwork' problem – here's what it's all about," October 18, 2017, https://www.businessinsider.com/what-is-karoshi-japanese-word-for-deathby-overwork-2017-10

[2] Leif Hetland from a sermon I heard, https://globalmissionawareness.com/

[3] Henry, M. (1994). Matthew Henry's commentary on the whole Bible: complete and unabridged in one volume (p. 1670). Peabody: Hendrickson.

[4] "To Lead Others, First Lead Yourself," Dr. John C. Maxwell, accessed, January 11, 2019. http://www.sermoncentral.com/articleb.asp?article=John-Maxwell-How-to-Lead-Yourself

ABOUT THE AUTHOR

Kent Murawski is a father, husband, author and the lead pastor of Journey Church in Cambridge, MA (jcboston.org). Journey Church is a young church in one of the most influential areas of the United States. Home to Harvard and MIT, Cambridge is like no other place on earth. It's an academic and political hotbed. To say Cambridge is influential is an understatement. Eight U.S. presidents have graduated from Harvard alone, and MIT boasts eighty-one Nobel-laureates! Kent blogs extensively about life, leadership and ministry (kentmurawski.com) and lives in Greater Boston with his wife, Gina, and their three children.

OTHER BOOKS BY KENT

The Transition: Thriving Spiritually from High School to College and Beyond

God's plan for you is not just to survive college. He wants you to thrive and flourish in your relationship with Him, to see the world through His eyes, and to tap into the creative power of His Spirit to change the world around you, not just maintain status quo.

For descriptions on all Kent's titles, please visit
www.kentmurawski.com/books.